THE CANADIAN LIVING
COOKING
COLLECTION

GREAT
DESSERTS

The following Canadian companies were involved in the production
of this Collection: Colour Technologies, Fred Bird & Associates Limited,
Gordon Sibley Design Inc., On-line Graphics, Telemedia Publishing Inc. and
The Madison Book Group Inc.

We acknowledge the contribution of
Drew Warner, Joie Warner and Flavor Publications.

Produced by
The Madison Book Group Inc.
40 Madison Avenue
Toronto, Ontario
Canada
M5R 2S1

GREAT DESSERTS

■ *On our cover:*
Chocolate Pâté (p. 11)

You'll find it easy to choose the perfect sweet ending for any meal with the 65 luscious desserts we've included here. There's something for every occasion, and for every season of the year — *Blueberry-Lemon Picnic Cake* or *Rhubarb Crisp* for those first outings in spring, cool *Raspberry Snow* or light-as-air *Fruit Shortcake* for the long hot days of summer, *Rustic Plum and Nectarine Tart* or *Apple Cranberry Raisin Pie* made with the first fruits of autumn, soul-warming *Cherry Crumble* or *Chocolate Bread Pudding with Grand Marnier Custard Sauce* in front of a winter fire. . .or rich 'n' creamy *White Chocolate Cheesecake* any time!

Great Desserts is just one of the eight full-color cookbooks that make up THE CANADIAN LIVING COOKING COLLECTION. Inside each of these colorful cookbooks are the kind of satisfying, easy-to-make dishes you'll want to cook over and over again. Each recipe in the Collection has been carefully selected and tested by *Canadian Living* to make sure it turns out wonderfully every time you make it. When you collect all eight cookbooks, you can choose from over 500 dishes — from marvelous soups to sensational desserts — all guaranteed to make any meal extra special.

Elizabeth Baird

Elizabeth Baird
Food Director, *Canadian Living* Magazine

Meringue Glacée en Surprise

A ring of chocolate adds to the complex flavors of this dessert. The meringues mixed with the cream add intriguing texture.

6 oz	semisweet chocolate, melted	175 g
2 cups	whipping cream	500 mL
1/4 cup	icing sugar	50 mL
1/4 cup	kirsch	50 mL
1	pkg (300 g) unsweetened frozen raspberries, thawed and drained	1
12	2-inch (5 cm) meringue shells	12
	SAUCE	
1	pkg (300 g) unsweetened frozen raspberries	1
2 tbsp	icing sugar	25 mL
2 tbsp	kirsch	25 mL
	GARNISH (optional)	
	Raspberries	

■ Line sides of 10-inch (3 L) springform pan with parchment paper, pinning edges of paper together. Paint parchment paper with chocolate. Refrigerate until set, about 10 minutes. Paint with second coat of chocolate; refrigerate until set.

■ In large bowl, whip cream; beat in icing sugar and kirsch. Fold in raspberries. Crush meringue shells finely; fold into raspberry mixture. Spoon into chocolate shell and smooth top. Cover with foil; freeze for 5 hours or until firm. Remove sides from pan; peel off paper. Slide dessert onto serving plate.

■ **Sauce:** In food processor or blender, purée raspberries, icing sugar and kirsch; strain through sieve to remove seeds. Cut dessert into wedges and serve with sauce. Garnish with raspberries if desired. Makes 8 servings.

RASPBERRY SNOW
The zippy flavor of raspberry gives kids a refreshing cool lift on a summer day. Combine 1-1/2 cups (375 mL) water and 3/4 cup (175 mL) frozen raspberry juice concentrate, thawed; pour into ice cube tray and freeze. In food processor, process half of the frozen raspberry cubes until finely crushed. Repeat with remaining cubes. Spoon into paper cups or bowls and serve with spoons. Makes 6 to 8 servings.

Meringue Glacée en Surprise ▶

Polynesian Bombe

Change the flavors of this bombe with different ices. The sauces should contrast in color and complement in taste.

2 cups	mango ice, softened	500 mL
2 cups	raspberry ice, softened	500 mL
2 cups	lime ice, softened	500 mL
	KIWI & CRÈME DE MENTHE SAUCE	
4	kiwifruit, peeled	4
1/3 cup	orange juice	75 mL
1/4 cup	granulated sugar	50 mL
1 tbsp	crème de menthe	15 mL
	STRAWBERRY & GRAND MARNIER SAUCE	
2 cups	strawberries	500 mL
1/4 cup	granulated sugar	50 mL
1/4 cup	Grand Marnier	50 mL
	APRICOT & KIRSCH SAUCE	
1 cup	drained canned apricots	250 mL
1/2 cup	orange juice	125 mL
2 tbsp	kirsch	25 mL

■ Spread mango ice around sides of 6-cup (1.5 L) bowl, preferably stainless steel; freeze for 30 minutes. Spread raspberry ice over mango ice; freeze again for 30 minutes. Spoon lime ice into centre and smooth top. Cover with foil; freeze for 5 hours or until firm.

■ **Kiwi & Crème de Menthe Sauce:** In food processor or blender, purée kiwifruit, orange juice, sugar and crème de menthe. Strain through sieve to remove seeds if desired.

■ **Strawberry & Grand Marnier Sauce:** In food processor or blender, purée strawberries. Strain through sieve to remove seeds. Stir in sugar and Grand Marnier.

■ **Apricot & Kirsch Sauce:** In food processor or blender, purée apricots, orange juice and kirsch.

■ Dip mould into hot water to unmould. Let soften slightly for 30 minutes in refrigerator. On individual plates, spoon some of each sauce in attractive design. Cut bombe and place slices on top. Makes about 6 servings.

Christmas Bombe with Whisky Sauce

Try different color combinations of ice cream for attractive results. Brandy or orange juice can be used instead of whisky for the sauce.

1 cup	mincemeat	250 mL
4 cups	vanilla ice cream, softened	1 L
2 cups	strawberry ice cream, softened	500 mL
2 cups	chocolate or coffee ice cream, softened	500 mL
	WHISKY SAUCE	
1/2 cup	butter	125 mL
1 cup	granulated sugar	250 mL
1	egg	1
1/2 cup	whisky	125 mL

■ In large bowl, fold mincemeat into 2 cups (500 mL) of the vanilla ice cream; reserve in freezer. Spread remaining vanilla ice cream around sides of 8-cup (2 L) bowl, preferably stainless steel. Freeze for 30 minutes.

■ Spread strawberry ice cream over vanilla; freeze for 30 minutes. Repeat with chocolate ice cream. Spoon mincemeat mixture into centre; smooth top. Cover with foil; freeze for 5 hours or until firm.

■ **Whisky Sauce:** In heavy saucepan, melt butter. Stir together sugar and egg; add to butter and cook gently over medium heat for 2 to 3 minutes or until sugar has dissolved. Let cool to room temperature. Stir in whisky.

■ Dip mould into hot water to unmould onto serving plate. Let soften slightly for 30 minutes in refrigerator. Pour half of the Whisky Sauce over bombe; pass remaining sauce separately. Makes about 8 servings.

Strawberry Cheese Dip

Serve this with chunks of fresh fruit, such as pineapple, melon, apples, pears, peaches, grapes or nectarines. If fresh strawberries are not available for the dip, substitute 1/4 cup (50 mL) strawberry jam.

1/4 lb	cream cheese, softened	125 g	
1/2 cup	sour cream	125 mL	
1/2 cup	puréed fresh strawberries	125 mL	
2 tbsp	packed brown sugar	25 mL	
1 tbsp	lemon juice	15 mL	
	Fresh fruit chunks		

■ In blender or food processor, combine cream cheese, sour cream, strawberries, sugar and lemon juice; process until blended. Pour into serving dish and chill; serve with chunks of fresh fruit. Makes about 1-1/2 cups (375 mL).

Frozen Zabaglione

This dessert can also be made with white wine instead of Marsala; call it a sabayon instead. Serve with amaretti biscuits (see Muffins and Cookies, *p. 47) or tuiles.*

6	egg yolks	6
1/2 cup	granulated sugar	125 mL
3/4 cup	Marsala wine	175 mL
1-1/2 cups	whipping cream	375 mL
	SAUCE	
1	can (14 oz/398 mL) peaches, drained	1
2 tbsp	amaretto	25 mL
	Juice and grated rind of 1 lemon	
1/4 cup	slivered almonds	50 mL
	GARNISH	
6 to 8	strawberries	6 to 8

■ In heavy saucepan, whisk egg yolks with sugar over low heat until light and fluffy. Whisk in Marsala and cook gently, whisking until mixture has tripled in volume. Remove from heat and let cool slightly.

■ Whip cream; fold into egg mixture. Spoon into 9- × 5-inch (2 L) loaf pan. Cover with foil and freeze for 5 hours or until firm.

■ **Sauce:** In blender or food processor, purée peaches, amaretto and lemon juice. Fold in lemon rind and slivered almonds.

■ **Garnish:** Cut strawberries through to stem several times, leaving each berry intact. Fan out.

■ To serve, spoon sauce onto individual plates. Place slice of zabaglione on top. Decorate with strawberries. Makes 6 to 8 servings.

Frozen Raspberry Cream

This tangy dessert can be prepared in five minutes, then frozen until firm. If it's made a day or more in advance, remove it from the freezer at least 15 minutes before serving.

1	pkg (15 oz/425 g) frozen raspberries	1
1	can (12-1/2 oz/355 mL) frozen pink lemonade concentrate	1
4 cups	vanilla ice cream, slightly softened	1 L

■ In food processor fitted with metal blade, process frozen raspberries until slushy. Add frozen lemonade concentrate; process with on/off motion until mixed.

■ In large bowl, stir raspberry mixture into ice cream until combined. Cover and freeze until firm, about 3 hours. Makes 8 to 10 servings.

Orange Zabaglione

Orange juice and liqueur are a change from the traditional Marsala in this light and frothy Italian dessert.

6	egg yolks	6
1/3 cup	orange juice	75 mL
1/3 cup	orange liqueur	75 mL
3 tbsp	granulated sugar	50 mL

■ In top of nonaluminum double boiler over simmering water, whisk together egg yolks, orange juice, liqueur and sugar; cook, whisking constantly, until tripled in volume and thickened slightly, about 10 minutes. Serve immediately in stemmed glasses. Makes 6 servings.

> *NUTTY MAPLE WHIP*
> *This dessert is satisfying and light, yet so simple that children can make it in minutes. In bowl, blend 3 cups (750 mL) yogurt with 1/2 cup (125 mL) maple syrup; stir in 1/2 cup (125 mL) chopped peanuts, almonds or pecans. Sprinkle with crumbled maple-flavored cookies if desired. Serve immediately. Makes about 4 servings.*

Meringue Trifle

A centrepiece dessert, this inventive trifle combines the classic tastes of ripe bananas and rich chocolate. You can freeze the crumbled meringues ahead of time, but assemble the trifle no longer than 4 hours before serving.

2 cups	whipping cream	500 mL
3 tbsp	icing sugar	50 mL
3 tbsp	orange liqueur	50 mL
6 oz	semisweet chocolate	175 g
2 tbsp	butter	25 mL
3	bananas	3

	MERINGUE	
4	egg whites	4
Pinch	cream of tartar	Pinch
1 cup	granulated sugar	250 mL
1/2 tsp	vanilla	2 mL

> **FROZEN BANANA POPS**
>
> *Children will enjoy making their own summer treats, especially when they're this delicious and this easy. Cut 2 peeled ripe bananas into thirds; insert wooden stick. Spread 1 tbsp (15 mL) honey over banana pieces and roll in 1/4 cup (50 mL) chopped peanuts. Wrap in plastic wrap and freeze. Makes 6 servings.*

■ **Meringues:** In bowl, beat egg whites with cream of tartar until soft peaks form; gradually beat in sugar until stiff peaks form. Beat in vanilla.

■ Onto foil-lined baking sheet, spoon mixture into 2-inch (5 cm) rounds. Bake in 250°F (120°C) oven for 2 hours. Let cool; break each round into 3 or 4 pieces. Set aside.

■ In bowl, whip cream; gradually beat in sugar. Fold in orange liqueur. In top of double boiler over hot, not boiling, water, or in microwaveable dish, melt chocolate with butter; let cool slightly. Cut bananas into 1/2-inch (1 cm) thick slices.

■ Spoon one-third of the whipped cream into 8- to 10-cup (2 to 2.5 L) serving bowl. Cover with one-third of the meringue pieces; drizzle with one-third of the chocolate. Cover with half of the bananas. Repeat with whipped cream, meringues, chocolate and bananas. Top with remaining whipped cream, then meringues, then chocolate. Refrigerate until serving. Makes 8 to 10 servings.

Chocolate Pâté

For a more spirited flavor, add another tablespoon (15 mL) of rum. If serving the loaf whole, drizzle Chocolate Sauce over top before slicing. For our cover photograph, we sliced the loaf into individual servings and swirled the Chocolate Sauce into the Crème Anglaise.

12 oz	semisweet chocolate, chopped	375 g
1-3/4 cups	whipping cream	425 mL
1 tbsp	rum	15 mL
	Crème Anglaise and Chocolate Sauce (optional) (recipes follow)	
	Icing sugar	

■ Line 8- × 4-inch (1.5 L) loaf pan with plastic wrap; set aside.

■ In bowl, set over hot, not boiling, water, melt chocolate; let cool completely, stirring occasionally.

■ In separate bowl, whip cream with rum; whisk one-quarter into chocolate. Fold in remaining whipped cream. Spoon into prepared pan and smooth top. Cover and refrigerate for 4 hours or until firm or for up to 3 days.

■ To serve, unmould pâté; remove plastic wrap. Cut into 1/2-inch (1 cm) thick slices; place on dessert plates. Spoon 3 tbsp (50 mL) Crème Anglaise around each serving if using. Sprinkle with droplets of Chocolate Sauce if using. Using toothpick or skewer, swirl chocolate to make attractive pattern. Dust lightly with icing sugar. Makes 12 servings.

CRÈME ANGLAISE

4	egg yolks	4
1/3 cup	granulated sugar	75 mL
2 cups	milk	500 mL
1 tbsp	vanilla	15 mL

■ In bowl, whisk together egg yolks and sugar. In saucepan, heat milk just until bubbles form around edge; whisk one-third into egg yolk mixture.

■ Add egg yolk mixture to saucepan; cook over medium heat, stirring with wooden spoon, for 3 to 5 minutes or until thickened slightly and sauce coats back of spoon. Do not boil.

■ Strain immediately through fine sieve; strain again if necessary to ensure silky consistency. Stir in vanilla. Place plastic wrap directly on surface; refrigerate until chilled or for up to 1 day. Makes 2 cups (500 mL).

CHOCOLATE SAUCE

1 cup	semisweet chocolate chips	250 mL
1/4 cup	corn syrup	50 mL
1/4 cup	milk	50 mL
1 tbsp	butter	15 mL
1 tsp	vanilla	5 mL

■ In saucepan, combine chocolate chips, corn syrup, milk and butter; heat over low heat, stirring occasionally, just until chocolate has melted. Stir in vanilla. Makes about 1 cup (250 mL).

Light Crème Brûlée

This version of a classic dessert has a praline topping.

1-1/2 cups	milk	375 mL
1 cup	light cream	250 mL
1	piece vanilla bean (about 4 inches/10 cm)	1
2	eggs	2
2	egg yolks	2
2 tbsp	granulated sugar	25 mL
1 tsp	cornstarch	5 mL
	Hazelnut Praline (recipe follows)	

■ In heavy saucepan, combine milk, cream and vanilla bean; cook over medium-low heat until bubbles form around edge of pan. Do not boil.

■ Meanwhile, place eggs and egg yolks in bowl. Combine sugar and cornstarch; beat into eggs. Gradually pour in hot milk mixture, stirring constantly. Return to pan and cook over medium-low heat, stirring, until thick enough to coat back of metal spoon. Strain into 4-cup (1 L) baking dish or 6 individual custard cups. Let cool, stirring occasionally; refrigerate for at least 6 hours or until firm.

■ About 2 hours before serving, evenly spread Hazelnut Praline over custard. Place on baking sheet and broil for 3 to 4 minutes or until praline is dark golden brown. Refrigerate until chilled. Makes 6 servings.

HAZELNUT PRALINE

1/2 cup	granulated sugar	125 mL
2 tbsp	chopped toasted hazelnuts	25 mL

■ In small heavy saucepan, heat sugar over medium heat, without stirring but shaking pan occasionally, for about 3 minutes or until sugar has melted and is golden. Sprinkle nuts onto buttered plate and pour syrup over. Let cool until hardened; break into pieces. Process in food processor until finely ground, or place in heavy plastic bag and crush with rolling pin.

Pear Melba

Here's a delightful variation of the classic peach melba. Be sure to use juicy ripe pears or, of course, you can use peaches.

1/3 cup	orange juice	75 mL
2 tsp	cornstarch	10 mL
1	pkg (300 g) frozen raspberries, thawed	1
1 tsp	grated lemon rind	5 mL
1 tbsp	lemon juice	15 mL
4	large pears	4
	Vanilla ice cream	

■ In small saucepan, combine orange juice and cornstarch. Add raspberries, lemon rind and juice; cook over medium heat until slightly thickened, about 2 minutes. Remove from heat and let cool to room temperature.

■ Peel, core and cut pears into wedges. Place scoop of ice cream in each serving dish; surround with pear wedges and spoon sauce over. Makes 4 servings.

STRAWBERRIES WITH VANILLA YOGURT
Summer-fresh flavors couldn't be more evident than in this easy dessert. Depending upon the sweetness of the berries, you may want to add a little more sugar. Divide 2 cups (500 mL) sliced strawberries among 4 dessert dishes. Combine 1 cup (250 mL) plain yogurt, 1 tbsp (15 mL) packed brown sugar and 1/2 tsp (1 mL) vanilla; dollop over berries. Makes 4 servings.

Rustic Plum and Nectarine Tart

Serve this with whipped cream or custard sauce. You can substitute peaches for the nectarines or make the tart entirely with plums.

1/2 cup	(approx) granulated sugar	125 mL
1/3 cup	toasted pecans*	75 mL
1/4 cup	all-purpose flour	50 mL
1-1/4 lb	plums, quartered (about 14)	625 g
1/2 lb	nectarines, cut in wedges (about 3)	250 g
1 tbsp	butter	15 mL
1 tbsp	milk or cream	15 mL
3 tbsp	red currant jelly or sieved apricot jam	50 mL
	PASTRY	
2 cups	all-purpose flour	500 mL
1 tbsp	granulated sugar	15 mL
1/2 tsp	salt	2 mL
1/3 cup	cold butter, cubed	75 mL
1/3 cup	cold lard, cubed	75 mL
1	egg yolk	1
1 tsp	lemon juice	5 mL
	Ice water	

■ **Pastry:** In large bowl, combine flour, sugar and salt; cut in butter and lard until mixture resembles fine crumbs with a few larger pieces.

■ In measuring cup, beat together egg yolk, lemon juice and enough ice water to make 1/2 cup (125 mL); briskly stir enough into flour mixture, 1 tbsp (15 mL) at a time, to make dough hold together. Shape into disc; wrap and chill for at least 20 minutes.

■ Let cold pastry stand for 15 minutes at room temperature before rolling. On lightly floured surface, roll out pastry into 14-inch (35 cm) circle, leaving edges rough. Transfer to 12-inch (30 cm) pizza pan, letting pastry hang over edge.

■ In food processor, process 1/4 cup (50 mL) of the sugar, pecans and flour until nuts are finely ground; spread over pastry on pan. Arrange plums and nectarines over nuts; sprinkle with remaining 1/4 cup (50 mL) sugar. Dot with butter.

■ Fold pastry overhang over fruit. Brush milk over pastry; sprinkle with a little sugar. Bake in 425°F (220°C) oven for 15 minutes. Reduce heat to 375°F (190°C) and bake for 35 minutes longer or until pastry is golden and juices are bubbling, shielding pastry with foil to prevent over-browning if necessary. Let cool. Melt jelly and brush over fruit. Makes 10 to 12 servings.

*To toast pecans, bake on baking sheet in 350°F (180°C) oven for about 5 minutes or until golden.

Perfect Pastry Every Time

Even experienced pie makers use this never-fail recipe. When measuring the flour, spoon it into a dry measure and level with a knife.

6 cups	cake-and-pastry flour (or 5-1/4 cups/1.3 L all-purpose flour)	1.5 L
1-1/2 tsp	salt	7 mL
2-1/3 cups	lard or shortening (1 lb/454 g)	575 mL
1	egg	1
1 tbsp	white vinegar	15 mL
	Ice water	

■ In large bowl, combine flour with salt. Using pastry blender or two knives, cut in lard until mixture resembles fine crumbs with a few larger pieces. In measuring cup and using fork, beat together egg and vinegar; add enough ice water to make 1 cup (250 mL).

■ Stirring briskly with fork, gradually add just enough egg mixture, 1 tbsp (15 mL) at a time, to flour mixture to make dough hold together.

■ Divide into 6 portions; press each into ball. Wrap in plastic wrap and refrigerate for at least 20 minutes or for up to 1 week, or freeze for up to 3 months. Let cold pastry stand for 15 minutes at room temperature before rolling out. Makes enough for six 9-inch (23 cm) single-crust pie shells or 3 double-crust pies.

---

5 STEPS TO PERFECT FRUIT PIES

1. Line 9-inch (23 cm) pie plate with pastry.
2. In large bowl, combine prepared fruit, sugar, flour, 1 tbsp (15 mL) lemon juice and flavoring (see Pie Chart, opposite page).
3. Fill pastry shell with fruit mixture; dot filling with 1 tbsp (15 mL) butter.
4. Moisten edge of bottom crust; cover with top crust. Trim and flute edges; cut steam vents. Brush top with milk or cream; sprinkle lightly with granulated sugar.
5. Bake in 425°F (220°C) oven for 15 minutes; reduce heat to 350°F (180°C) and bake for 45 to 60 minutes longer or until fruit is tender, filling thickened and crust golden.
• You can also freeze well-wrapped unbaked fruit pies for up to 4 months, with
the following changes: increase the amount of flour in each pie by 1 tbsp (15 mL) and don't cut steam vents until just before baking. Bake still-frozen pies in 450°F (230°C) oven for 15 minutes; reduce heat to 375°F (190°C) and bake for up to 60 minutes longer or until filling is thickened and crust golden brown.
• If you don't have time to bake pies now, you can freeze fruit without sugar in the quantities needed for pies (see Pie Chart, opposite page), then thaw just enough to separate. Make pies following the 5 Steps to Perfect Fruit Pies, increasing flour by 1 tbsp (15 mL), then bake for up to 60 minutes. If fruit has been frozen with sugar, subtract the amount of sugar in the fruit from the amount of sugar you add to the pie.

Perfect Processor Pastry

This food processor pastry will become a favorite in your kitchen.

3 cups	all-purpose flour	750 mL
1 tsp	salt	5 mL
1/2 cup	cold butter, cubed	125 mL
1/2 cup	cold lard, cubed	125 mL
1	egg	1
2 tsp	white vinegar	10 mL
	Ice water	

■ In food processor fitted with metal blade, combine flour and salt; process to mix. Using on/off motion, cut in butter and lard until mixture resembles fine crumbs with a few larger pieces.

■ In measuring cup, beat egg until foamy; add vinegar and enough ice water to make 2/3 cup (150 mL). With motor running, add egg mixture all at once; process just until dough starts to clump together and form ball.

■ Remove and divide into 3 portions; press into balls. Wrap in plastic wrap and chill for at least 30 minutes or for up to 3 days, or freeze for up to 3 months. Let cold pastry stand for 15 minutes at room temperature before rolling out. Makes enough for three 9-inch (23 cm) single-crust pie shells.

PIE CHART FOR DOUBLE-CRUST FRUIT PIES

Type of Pie	Prepared Fruit	Granulated Sugar	All-purpose Flour	Flavorings
Blueberry	4 cups (1 L)	2/3 cup (150 mL)	3 tbsp (50 mL)	1 tsp (5 mL) grated lemon rind
Peach	5 cups (1.25 L), peeled and sliced	3/4 cup (175 mL)	1/4 cup (50 mL)	2 tbsp (25 mL) chopped candied ginger
Plum	5 cups (1.25 L), quartered if large, halved if small	1 cup (250 mL)	1/4 cup (50 mL)	1/2 tsp (2 mL) cinnamon
Raspberry	4 cups (1 L)	1 cup (250 mL)	3 tbsp (50 mL)	none
Sour cherry	4 cups (1 L), pitted	1 cup (250 mL)	1/4 cup (50 mL)	1/2 tsp (2 mL) almond extract

Cherry Strudel

Phyllo pastry is not difficult to handle but you must work quickly to keep the sheets from drying out.

3 cups	sour cherries, pitted	750 mL
1/2 cup	granulated sugar	125 mL
2 tbsp	quick-cooking tapioca	25 mL
1 cup	cake crumbs or fresh bread crumbs	250 mL
1/2 cup	ground almonds	125 mL
6	sheets phyllo pastry	6
1/2 cup	melted butter	125 mL
2 tbsp	sliced almonds (optional)	25 mL
	Icing sugar	
	Whipped cream or ice cream (optional)	

■ In bowl, toss together cherries, granulated sugar and tapioca; set aside. Combine cake crumbs and ground almonds; set aside.

■ Place 1 of the phyllo sheets on damp tea towel, keeping remaining phyllo covered with waxed paper and another damp towel to prevent drying out. Lightly brush with butter; sprinkle evenly with 2 tbsp (25 mL) of the crumb mixture. Place second sheet on top; brush with butter and sprinkle with crumbs. Repeat with remaining pastry, butter and crumbs.

■ Stir cherry mixture and spoon over pastry, leaving 1-1/2-inch (4 cm) border on long edges and one short edge. Fold uncovered end and sides over filling. Starting at folded short end, roll up strudel jelly-roll fashion, using tea towel to help lift and roll pastry if necessary. Place seam side down on buttered jelly roll pan. Brush lightly with butter. Cut 4 horizontal slits, evenly spaced, in top of strudel.

■ Bake in 400°F (200°C) oven for 30 to 35 minutes or until pastry is crisp and golden, sprinkling with sliced almonds (if using) during last 5 minutes. Dust with icing sugar while still warm. Serve with whipped cream or ice cream if desired. Makes 8 to 10 servings.

CHERRIES JUBILATION

The two most common varieties of cherries you'll find are luscious, garnet red Bings and bright scarlet Montmorencies. Mellow and rich-tasting, Bing cherries can be eaten just as they are or in fresh fruit salads. Halved and pitted, laced with liqueur or plain, they're delicious folded into creamy fillings or whipped cream, then sandwiched between layers of chocolate cake. Bings can also be used to make splendid sauces for ice cream. Montmorencies, a little too tangy for eating out-of-hand, make the most mouthwatering pies, strudels, baked desserts, jams and jellies.

• Montmorencies are the best choice for bulk freezing. Save fridge space by spreading the cherries in single layers in a large pan, separating layers with paper towels. To freeze, wash and pit cherries; combine with half a pound (250 g) of sugar for every five pounds (2.5 kg) of pitted fruit. Bing cherries can be frozen unpitted and without sugar.

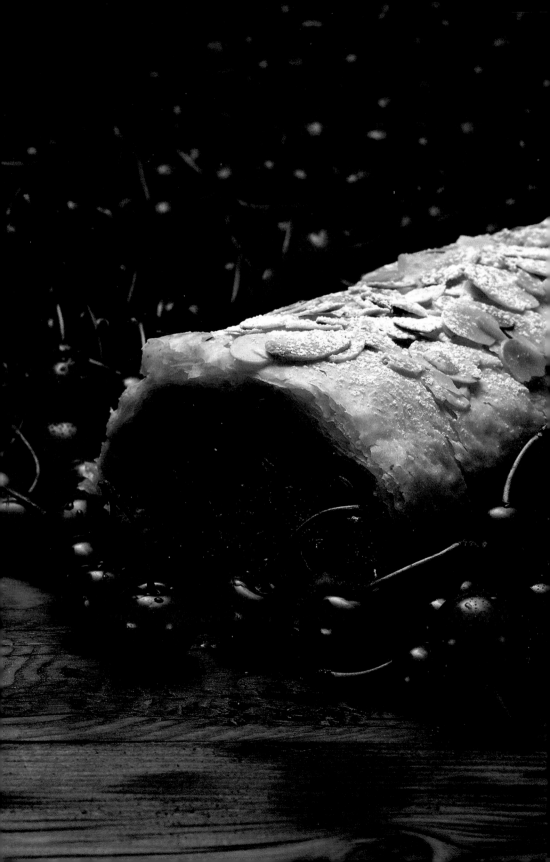

Peach Angel Pie

Delicate and delectable, this pie is fabulous when made with tree-ripened juicy peaches. Or substitute eight juicy apricots when they're in season. This pie cannot be frozen, but both the filling and the pie shell can be made ahead, then assembled just before serving.

4	ripe peaches, peeled and pitted	4
1	can (300 mL) sweetened condensed milk	1
1-1/2 tsp	unflavored gelatin	7 mL
1/4 cup	lemon juice	50 mL
1/4 tsp	almond extract	1 mL
1/2 cup	whipping cream, whipped	125 mL

	MERINGUE SHELL	
4	egg whites	4
3/4 cup	instant dissolving (fruit/berry) sugar	175 mL
1 tsp	vinegar	5 mL
1/2 tsp	almond extract	1 mL

	GARNISH	
1/4 cup	toasted slivered almonds	50 mL
2	peaches	2
1 tbsp	lemon juice	15 mL

■ In blender or food processor, purée peaches; blend in milk. Transfer to bowl.

■ In small nonaluminum bowl, sprinkle gelatin over lemon juice; place in pan of hot water over low heat and stir until gelatin is dissolved. Stir into peach purée along with almond extract; fold in whipped cream. Cover and refrigerate for 3 hours or up to 24 hours.

■ **Meringue Shell:** In bowl, beat egg whites until soft peaks form; gradually beat in sugar until stiff peaks form. Beat in vinegar and almond extract. Spoon into buttered 9- or 10-inch (23 or 25 cm) pie plate, spreading up sides of pan. Bake in 275°F (140°C) oven for about 1 hour or until golden and slightly dry. Let cool on rack.

■ Spoon filling into shell; garnish with almond slivers. Peel, pit and slice peaches, sprinkling with lemon juice as you cut; arrange on top of pie.

Apple Cranberry Raisin Pie

Plump ruby cranberries and crisp Spartan or Northern Spy apples combine to make one of the tastiest of fruit pies. This pie can be frozen.

	Pastry for double-crust 9-inch (23 cm) pie	
2 cups	cranberries	500 mL
1-1/2 cups	granulated sugar	375 mL
1/4 cup	water	50 mL
1 tsp	cinnamon	5 mL
1/4 tsp	salt	1 mL
3	large apples, peeled and sliced	3
1 cup	seedless raisins	250 mL
2 tbsp	cornstarch	25 mL

SPICES AND FLAVORINGS FOR PIES
Cinnamon is traditional in apple pie, while the other fruits are usually used without spicing. But for a change, enhance any fruit with a generous pinch of cinnamon, nutmeg or mace. Peach is delicious with a little chopped preserved ginger; cherry with a few drops of almond extract. Grated orange rind perks up plum, apple or cranberry. For extra flavor, add a spoonful of rum or fruit liqueur. Raisins, toasted almonds or chopped pecans can also make interesting additions to fruit pie fillings.

■ On lightly floured surface, roll out half of the pastry and line 9-inch (23 cm) pie plate.

■ In saucepan, combine cranberries, sugar, 2 tbsp (25 mL) of the water, cinnamon and salt; cook over medium heat for about 10 minutes or until cranberries pop. Stir in apple slices and raisins.

■ Combine cornstarch and remaining water; blend into cranberry mixture. Cook, stirring, for about 5 minutes or until thickened slightly.

■ Spoon filling into pastry-lined pie plate. Roll out remaining pastry and place on top of pie, leaving 1-inch (2.5 cm) overhang. Trim edges. Tuck overhang under bottom crust and press together to form rim; flute rim. Cut steam vents in top of pie; bake in 400°F (200°C) oven for about 35 minutes or until crust is golden.

Open-Face Apple Pie

Glaze apple slices with apricot jam for a delicious variation on standard apple pie. Use apples that hold their shape when cooked, such as Golden Delicious.

	Pastry for 9-inch (23 cm) flan pan	
6	large apples	6
1 tbsp	lemon juice	15 mL
1/4 cup	granulated sugar	50 mL
1/2 cup	raisins	125 mL
1 tbsp	butter, melted	15 mL
1/2 cup	apricot jam	125 mL

■ On lightly floured surface, roll out pastry and fit into 9-inch (23 cm) pan; flute edge.

Peel and core apples; cut into 1/4-inch (5 mm) thick slices to make about 6 cups (1.5 L). Toss with lemon juice; add sugar and toss again.

■ Arrange 2 layers of slightly overlapping apple slices in circles in pastry shell. Scatter raisins over top; drizzle with butter. Bake near bottom of 400°F (200°C) oven for about 35 minutes or until apples are tender and crust is golden brown.

■ In small saucepan, heat jam until melted; spoon evenly over apples. Bake for about 5 minutes longer or until apples are glazed.

Fresh Peach Crumb Pie

As easy to make as it is good to eat, this pie with its pat-in crumb crust will have special appeal for those who love homemade pies but are unsure of their pastry-making skills.

1-1/2 cups	all-purpose flour	375 mL
1/2 cup	granulated sugar	125 mL
1/4 tsp	cinnamon (optional)	1 mL
Pinch	salt	Pinch
1/2 cup	butter, softened	125 mL
	FILLING	
4 cups	sliced peeled peaches (about 10)	1 L
1 tbsp	lemon juice	15 mL
1/2 cup	granulated sugar	125 mL
2 tbsp	cornstarch	25 mL

■ In bowl, stir together flour, sugar, cinnamon (if using) and salt; cut in butter until mixture is

crumbly. Set 3/4 cup (175 mL) aside for topping. Press remaining crumbs onto bottom and 3/4 inch (2 cm) up side of 9-inch (2.5 L) springform pan. Place on baking sheet and bake in 425°F (220°C) oven for 5 minutes.

■ **Filling:** In bowl, combine peaches and lemon juice. Stir together sugar and cornstarch; sprinkle over peaches and stir gently to combine. Arrange peach mixture in prepared shell. Bake in 400°F (200°C) oven for 40 minutes. Sprinkle with reserved crumbs; bake for 5 minutes longer or until crumbs are nicely browned and filling is tender and bubbling. Serve warm or cold.

Open-Face Apple Pie ▶

Fresh Fruit Dumplings

Depending on the season, choose large peaches, crisp tart apples, nectarines or large purple or red plums for this delicious dessert. The pastry is a variation on a pâte brisée and is wonderful for fruit tarts as well as dumplings.

CREAM CHEESE PASTRY

1/2 cup	butter	125 mL
4 oz	cream cheese	125 g
1/4 cup	granulated sugar	50 mL
1	egg	1
1-3/4 cups	all-purpose flour	425 mL

FILLING

6	large peaches or nectarines, peeled and pitted	6
1/3 cup	lightly packed brown sugar	75 mL
1/4 cup	raisins	50 mL
2 tbsp	butter, softened	25 mL
1/2 tsp	cinnamon	2 mL
1/4 tsp	cloves	1 mL

SYRUP

1 cup	packed brown sugar	250 mL
2/3 cup	boiling water	150 mL
1/4 cup	maple syrup	50 mL
1 tbsp	lemon juice	15 mL

GARNISH (Optional)

Whipped cream

■ **Cream Cheese Pastry:** In bowl, cream butter and cheese with sugar; add egg and beat well. Blend in flour. Gather dough into ball; wrap and chill for 1 hour. Roll out pastry into 12- × 9-inch (30 × 23 cm) rectangle about 1/8 inch (3 mm) thick. Cut into 6 squares.

■ **Filling:** Place 1 whole peach on each square. Mix together sugar, raisins, butter, cinnamon and cloves; divide among peaches, spooning into cavity. Bring corners of pastry up over fruit and pinch together to seal. Place dumplings in 13- × 9-inch (3.5 L) baking dish.

■ **Syrup:** In saucepan, heat together sugar, boiling water and maple syrup, stirring until sugar dissolves. Add lemon juice; pour over dumplings.

■ Bake in 400°F (200°C) oven, basting with syrup a few times, for 35 to 45 minutes or until crust is golden and fruit is tender. Serve warm or cold, garnished with whipped cream if desired. Makes 6 servings.

Peach Dessert Pizza

This dessert is easy to make and attractive to serve. Although it's not really a pizza, it looks like one. Keep it refrigerated until serving time.

1/2 cup	butter	125 mL
1/4 cup	icing sugar	50 mL
1 cup	all-purpose flour	250 mL
	FILLING	
2 tbsp	peach or apricot jam, melted	25 mL
1/4 lb	cream cheese	125 g
1/2 cup	whipping cream	125 mL
1 tsp	grated orange rind	5 mL
6	peaches, peeled, pitted and sliced	6
	GLAZE	
2/3 cup	orange juice	150 mL
1/2 cup	peach or apricot jam	125 mL
2 tbsp	cornstarch	25 mL
2 tbsp	packed brown sugar	25 mL
	GARNISH	
1/2 cup	whipping cream	125 mL
	Granulated sugar	

■ In food processor or in bowl with pastry blender, combine butter, icing sugar and flour until mixture holds together when pressed with fingers. Pat into 12-inch (30 cm) pizza pan; prick all over with fork. Bake in 350°F (180°C) oven for 15 to 20 minutes or until lightly browned; let cool.

■ **Filling:** Brush crust with melted jam to seal. In bowl, beat together cream cheese, whipping cream and orange rind; spread over crust. Attractively arrange peach slices on top.

■ **Glaze:** In small saucepan, blend together orange juice, jam, cornstarch and brown sugar; cook, stirring constantly, until boiling, thickened and clear. Let cool slightly; spoon over peaches.

■ **Garnish:** Whip cream; add sugar to taste. Using pastry bag or spoon, pipe around edge of pizza. Makes 8 to 10 servings.

Spicy Pumpkin Cheesecake

This luscious cheesecake, flavored with cinnamon, nutmeg and allspice, is the perfect make-ahead dessert for a harvest dinner.

	CRUST	
2 cups	graham wafer crumbs	500 mL
2/3 cup	unsalted butter, melted	150 mL
3 tbsp	granulated sugar	50 mL
Pinch	each cinnamon and nutmeg	Pinch

	FILLING	
1 lb	cream cheese (at room temperature)	500 g
2/3 cup	granulated sugar	150 mL
1/4 cup	all-purpose flour	50 mL
6	eggs	6
2 cups	canned or fresh pumpkin purée	500 mL
1 tsp	cinnamon	5 mL
3/4 tsp	nutmeg	4 mL
1/4 tsp	allspice	1 mL

	GARNISH	
1 cup	whipping cream	250 mL
2 tbsp	icing sugar	25 mL
	Whole grapes or pecan halves (optional)	

■ **Crust:** In small bowl, mix together wafer crumbs, butter, sugar, cinnamon and nutmeg. Press onto bottom and side of 10-inch (3 L) springform pan. Refrigerate while making filling.

■ **Filling:** In large bowl, beat cream cheese with sugar until light and fluffy; beat in flour. Beat in eggs, one at a time, beating well after each addition. Stir in pumpkin purée, cinnamon, nutmeg and allspice; pour into prepared crust.

■ Bake in 350°F (180°C) oven for 1 hour and 15 minutes or just until barely firm to the touch. Run knife around edge of pan to loosen cake. Turn off heat and let cheesecake stand in oven for 30 minutes. Open oven door and let stand for 30 minutes longer.

■ Transfer cheesecake to wire rack and let cool for 1 hour. Cover and refrigerate for at least 2 hours or overnight.

■ **Garnish:** Whip cream; gradually beat in sugar. Place cheesecake on serving platter and remove side of pan. Garnish with rosettes of whipped cream, and grapes (if using). Makes 10 to 12 servings.

Summer Fruit Shortcake

Traditionally, fruit shortcakes are served on warm, split and buttered baking-powder biscuits. For a change, try these Lemon Biscuits. Use any seasonal fruit, such as strawberries, blueberries, blackberries, raspberries, red currants, plums and peaches.

3 cups	mixed fresh fruit	750 mL
3 tbsp	granulated sugar	50 mL
1 tbsp	lemon juice	15 mL
1 cup	strawberry purée	250 mL
1 cup	whipping cream, whipped	250 mL
	LEMON BISCUITS	
	Milk	
	Grated rind and juice of 1 lemon	
2 cups	all-purpose flour	500 mL
2 tbsp	(approx) granulated sugar	25 mL
4 tsp	baking powder	20 mL
1/2 tsp	salt	2 mL
2 tbsp	shortening	25 mL
2 tbsp	butter	25 mL

■ In bowl, sprinkle fruit with 2 tbsp (25 mL) of the sugar and lemon juice; toss to mix well. Set aside.

■ **Lemon Biscuits:** In measuring cup, add enough milk to lemon juice to make 2/3 cup (150 mL); stir and set aside for 15 minutes to sour.

■ In bowl, stir together flour, sugar, baking powder, salt and lemon rind; using pastry blender or two knives, cut in shortening and butter until well mixed. With fork, blend in soured milk to make soft dough. Don't overmix.

■ Turn out dough onto lightly floured surface; knead 6 to 8 times. Roll out or pat dough to 1/2-inch (1 cm) thickness. Using floured 3-inch (8 cm) round cutter, cut out 6 biscuits. Sprinkle lightly with more sugar. Bake on greased baking sheet in 425°F (220°C) oven for 12 to 15 minutes or until tops are browned. Let cool until warm; cut in half horizontally.

■ Spoon fruit mixture onto bottom halves of biscuits, reserving some fruit for garnish. Stir strawberry purée with remaining sugar; spoon over fruit mixture. Top with dollop of whipped cream, then biscuit tops. Garnish with more cream and remaining fruit. Makes 6 servings.

Apple Cheesecake

Sautéed apple slices make a nice texture contrast to the creamy filling.

1 cup	all-purpose flour	250 mL
1/4 cup	granulated sugar	50 mL
1 tbsp	grated lemon rind	15 mL
1	egg yolk	1
1/3 cup	butter, softened	75 mL
1/2 tsp	vanilla	2 mL
	FILLING	
3	apples (preferably Northern Spy)	3
1/4 cup	granulated sugar	50 mL
2 tbsp	butter	25 mL
2 tbsp	whipping cream	25 mL
1/2 lb	cream cheese	250 g
2/3 cup	packed brown sugar	150 mL
2	eggs	2
1-1/2 cups	sour cream	375 mL
1 tbsp	grated lemon rind	15 mL
1/3 cup	lemon juice	75 mL
1 tsp	vanilla	5 mL

■ In bowl, combine flour, sugar and lemon rind. Make well in centre and add egg yolk, butter and vanilla; blend into dry ingredients until in fine crumbs. (It will be fairly crumbly.) Pat onto bottom and 1/2 inch (1 cm) up side of greased 9-1/2-inch (2.5 L) springform pan. Bake in 325°F (160°C) oven for 12 to 15 minutes or until slightly golden.

■ **Filling:** Meanwhile, peel, core and halve apples; cut into 1/3-inch (8 mm) thick slices. In skillet, melt granulated sugar with butter over medium heat; cook apples for 3 to 5 minutes or just until tender (not mushy) and lightly browned. Add cream and cook, stirring occasionally, for 5 minutes or until apples are coated. Remove from heat; set aside.

■ In bowl, beat cream cheese with 1/2 cup (125 mL) of the brown sugar until smooth. Beat in eggs, one at a time. Beat in 1 cup (250 mL) of the sour cream, lemon rind and juice.

■ Using slotted spoon, arrange apples over crust; pour cheese mixture over and tap pan on counter to release air bubbles. Bake in 350°F (180°C) oven for 45 minutes or until sides are set but middle still jiggles slightly when pan is gently shaken. (There should be no cracks.)

■ Stir together remaining sour cream, brown sugar and vanilla; spread over hot cake and bake for 4 minutes. Run knife around inside edge of pan. Let cool to room temperature on rack; cover and refrigerate for several hours or overnight before removing side of pan. Makes about 8 servings.

White Chocolate Cheesecake

White chocolate makes a cheesecake even smoother and more luscious than normal. This cake freezes well.

	CRUST	
1-1/2 cups	chocolate wafer crumbs	375 mL
1/3 cup	butter, melted	75 mL

	FILLING	
8 oz	white chocolate	250 g
1 lb	cream cheese	500 g
1/2 cup	granulated sugar	125 mL
3	eggs	3
1 cup	sour cream	250 mL
1 tsp	grated orange rind	5 mL
1 tsp	vanilla	5 mL

	TOPPING	
1 cup	sour cream	250 mL
1 tbsp	granulated sugar	15 mL
1/2 tsp	vanilla	2 mL

	GARNISH	
	Chocolate curls*	
1 tbsp	icing sugar	15 mL

■ **Crust:** In bowl, combine wafer crumbs with butter; press into 9-inch (2.5 L) springform pan.

■ **Filling:** In top of double boiler over hot, not boiling, water, melt white chocolate; let cool for 5 minutes. Meanwhile, in large bowl, beat cream cheese with sugar until light. Beat in eggs, 1 at a time. Beat in white chocolate, sour cream, orange rind and vanilla. Pour over crust; bake in 350°F (180°C) oven for 40 to 45 minutes or until just set.

■ **Topping:** Combine sour cream, sugar and vanilla; spread over hot cake and return to oven for 3 to 5 minutes or until set. Immediately run knife around edge of cake to loosen. Let cool completely.

■ **Garnish:** Mound chocolate curls over cake; dust lightly with icing sugar. Chill. Makes 10 to 12 servings.

*To make chocolate curls: Use 6 oz (175 g) semisweet chocolate at room temperature. Hold chocolate in palm of hand until slightly softened but not melted. Using vegetable peeler, peel off curls, rewarming chocolate in palm of hand when necessary.

Chocolate Pecan Cake

The beauty of this glazed cake is that no one will ever know if the glaze isn't perfect! Allowing the glaze to run off onto the serving platter creates a stunning effect while covering any ragged edges. The white chocolate pattern on the topping hides any imperfections.

1-1/4 cups	pecans	300 mL
6 oz	semisweet chocolate, chopped	175 g
3/4 cup	unsalted butter, cubed	175 mL
3/4 cup	granulated sugar	175 mL
4	eggs, separated	4
2 tbsp	all-purpose flour	25 mL
1/4 tsp	cream of tartar	1 mL
	GLAZE	
8 oz	semisweet chocolate, chopped	250 g
1/2 cup	whipping cream	125 mL
3 oz	white chocolate	90 g

■ On baking sheet, bake pecans in 350°F (180°C) oven for 5 to 7 minutes or until fragrant; let cool. In food processor, finely chop pecans to make about 1 cup (250 mL); set aside.

■ In top of double boiler over hot, not boiling, water, melt chocolate with butter. In large bowl, beat 1/2 cup (125 mL) of the sugar with egg yolks until foamy; stir in chocolate mixture. Mix ground pecans with flour; stir into chocolate mixture.

■ In separate bowl, beat egg whites with cream of tartar until soft peaks form; gradually beat in remaining sugar until stiff peaks form.

■ Stir one-third of the egg whites into chocolate mixture; gently fold in remaining whites. Spoon mixture into buttered parchment paper-lined 9-inch (2.5 L) springform pan. Bake in 350°F (180°C) oven for 35 to 40 minutes or until tester inserted in centre comes out slightly moist and top of cake is firm. Let cake cool in pan. (Cake will be puffy and then fall.)

■ **Glaze:** In top of double boiler over hot, not boiling, water, heat dark chocolate with cream until smooth. Let cool until thickened but still spreadable.

■ Gently push down sides of cooled cake to even surface. Remove ring from pan. Invert cake onto rimmed serving platter large enough to leave 2-inch (5 cm) border around cake. Remove parchment paper and bottom of pan. Gently brush off any crumbs from top. *(Cake can be wrapped well and frozen for up to 4 months.)*

■ Carefully spread top and sides of cake with very thin layer of glaze. Reheat remaining glaze just until fluid and warm but not hot. Rotating cake slowly, pour glaze over cake to coat top and sides, letting glaze run onto platter right up to rim. Set aside.

■ In double boiler over hot, not boiling, water, melt white chocolate. Using pastry bag or parchment paper cone, pipe concentric circles over top of cake; pipe one or two circles around cake on glaze on platter. Pull tip of dull knife or end of chopstick through white chocolate circles to form patterns.

Oatmeal Spice Cake

The flavor of this easy-to-make moist and tender spice cake actually improves if you can keep it for a day.

2 cups	rolled oats	500 mL
2-1/2 cups	boiling water	625 mL
2-2/3 cups	all-purpose flour	650 mL
2 tsp	baking soda	10 mL
1-1/2 tsp	cinnamon	7 mL
1 tsp	salt	5 mL
1/2 tsp	nutmeg	2 mL
1 cup	butter (at room temperature)	250 mL
1-1/2 cups	packed brown sugar	375 mL
1-1/2 cups	granulated sugar	375 mL
4	eggs	4
2 tsp	vanilla	10 mL

TOPPING

1/2 cup	butter, melted	125 mL
1/3 cup	light cream	75 mL
1-1/2 cups	flaked coconut	375 mL
1 cup	packed brown sugar	250 mL
1 cup	chopped walnuts or pecans	250 mL

■ In bowl, cover rolled oats with boiling water; let stand for 1-1/2 hours or until completely cooled.

■ Combine flour, baking soda, cinnamon, salt and nutmeg; set aside.

■ In large mixing bowl, beat butter until creamy; beat in brown and granulated sugars until fluffy. Beat in eggs and vanilla; stir in cooled oat mixture, mixing well. Stir in dry ingredients, about a third at a time, to make stiff batter. Spread in greased and floured 13- × 9-inch (3.5 L) baking dish; bake in 350°F (180°C) oven for 50 to 60 minutes or until tester inserted in centre comes out clean.

■ **Topping:** Stir together butter and cream; blend in coconut, brown sugar and nuts; spread over baked cake. Broil until topping is bubbling, 2 to 3 minutes. Makes about 24 servings.

Upside-Down Pear Cake with Lemon Glaze

Here's a wonderful fresh fruit cake.

4	pears	4
2 tbsp	lemon juice	25 mL
3 tbsp	butter, softened	50 mL
3 tbsp	granulated sugar	50 mL
2 tbsp	(approx) sliced almonds	25 mL
1/2 cup	butter	125 mL
1/2 cup	granulated sugar	125 mL
2	eggs, beaten	2
1 tsp	grated lemon rind	5 mL
1/2 tsp	vanilla	2 mL
1 cup	cake-and-pastry flour	250 mL
1 tsp	baking powder	5 mL
1/2 tsp	salt	2 mL
2 tbsp	milk	25 mL
	Lemon Glaze (recipe follows)	

■ Peel and core pears. Cut lengthwise into thin slices, dropping slices into small bowl with lemon juice while cutting. Toss to coat; drain and set aside.

■ With 3 tbsp (50 mL) butter, grease side of 9-inch round (1.5 L) cake pan lightly; grease bottom generously. Sprinkle evenly with 3 tbsp (50 mL) sugar. Arrange almonds in 2 concentric circles on bottom of pan. Bake in 375°F (190°C) oven for 7 minutes or until bubbling and almonds are golden brown. Let cool.

■ Arrange largest pear slices in concentric circles in cake pan; place remaining slices on top. Reserve juice remaining in bowl.

■ In mixing bowl, cream 1/2 cup (125 mL) butter; beat in 1/2 cup (125 mL) sugar until pale and fluffy. Make 3 additions of beaten eggs, beating well after each addition. Stir in lemon rind, vanilla and 2 tbsp (25 mL) of the reserved juice.

■ Stir together flour, baking powder and salt; stir half of the mixture into batter, mixing well. Stir in milk, then remaining flour mixture to make stiff batter; spoon over pears and spread evenly.

■ Bake in 375°F (190°C) oven for 30 to 35 minutes or until golden brown and firm to the touch. Let stand for 5 minutes; invert onto plate. Pour Lemon Glaze evenly over cake (do not spread with knife). Serve at room temperature.

LEMON GLAZE

1/2 cup	granulated sugar	125 mL
2 tbsp	lemon juice	25 mL

■ In small heavy saucepan, combine sugar and lemon juice; cook over medium heat, stirring, just until sugar has dissolved. Increase heat to medium-high and boil, without stirring, until pale amber, brushing down any sugar crystals on side of pan with pastry brush dipped in water.

CAKES

Chocolate Snowball with Raspberry Sauce

If you don't have raspberry liqueur, or framboise, use orange liqueur. Instant dissolving sugar is finer than regular sugar and combines more easily with cold ingredients. If it's unavailable, process regular sugar in the food processor for 1 minute.

12 oz	semisweet chocolate, coarsely chopped	375 g
3/4 cup	thawed frozen raspberry juice concentrate	175 mL
1/2 cup	granulated sugar	125 mL
1 cup	unsalted butter, cubed	250 mL
6	eggs	6
1 tbsp	raspberry liqueur	15 mL
	TOPPING	
1 cup	whipping cream	250 mL
2 tbsp	raspberry liqueur	25 mL
1 tbsp	instant dissolving (fruit/berry) sugar	15 mL
1 tbsp	candied violets*	15 mL
	SAUCE	
2	pkg (each 300 g) individually frozen unsweetened raspberries, thawed	2
1/3 cup	instant dissolving (fruit/berry) sugar	75 mL
2 tbsp	raspberry liqueur	25 mL

■ Turn 8-cup (2 L) stainless steel mixing bowl upside down. Cut piece of heavy-duty foil large enough to cover outside of bowl; smooth foil over bowl. Remove foil (now in shape of bowl). Turn bowl right side up and place foil liner inside. Set aside.

■ In heavy saucepan, combine chocolate, raspberry juice concentrate and sugar over medium-low heat; cook, stirring constantly, just until chocolate has melted. Do not overheat. Remove from heat; whisk or beat in butter, then eggs, one at a time. Stir in liqueur.

■ Pour mixture into foil-lined bowl. Bake in 325°F (160°C) oven for 1 to 1-1/4 hours or until slightly puffed and top forms crust. Let cool to room temperature. Cover and refrigerate overnight. (You may have to push edges down slightly to even them off. Don't worry if centre falls.)

■ Invert onto serving platter; carefully remove bowl and peel off foil.

■ **Topping:** Whip cream; beat in liqueur and sugar. Using pastry bag fitted with rosette tip, pipe rosettes of whipped cream over cake. (Alternatively, spread cream over cake and swirl with knife.) Sprinkle with candied violets.

■ **Sauce:** Drain raspberries well, reserving juice. In food processor or blender, purée berries; strain through sieve into bowl to remove seeds. (Alternatively, push whole berries through food mill.) Stir in sugar and liqueur. (Thin sauce with a little of the reserved raspberry juice if necessary.)

■ To serve, pool some raspberry sauce on each plate. Slice snowball thinly; place slices on sauce. Makes 16 to 20 servings.
*Available in specialty food or confectionery stores.

Raisin-Cream Cheese Coffee Cake

This delicious orange-and-raisin coffee cake has cream cheese in it, which helps give it wonderful texture.

1-1/2 cups	raisins	375 mL
1/4 cup	orange liqueur or juice	50 mL
1 cup	butter, softened	250 mL
1	pkg (250 g) cream cheese	1
1-1/2 cups	packed brown sugar	375 mL
4	eggs	4
4 tsp	grated orange rind	20 mL
2 cups	all-purpose flour	500 mL
1 tbsp	baking powder	15 mL
1/2 tsp	salt	2 mL
1/2 tsp	nutmeg	2 mL
	Icing sugar	

■ In saucepan, combine raisins and liqueur; heat over low heat for 1 to 2 minutes or until plump and liquid is absorbed. Set aside.

■ In large bowl, beat butter, cream cheese and sugar until fluffy. Beat in eggs, one at a time; beat in rind.

■ Stir together flour, baking powder, salt and nutmeg; stir into batter in three additions, adding raisin mixture with last addition.

■ Spoon into greased and floured 9-inch (3 L) tube or Bundt pan; smooth top. Bake in 300°F (150°C) oven for about 80 minutes or until tester inserted into middle comes out clean. Let cool in pan for 5 minutes. Turn out onto rack; let cool completely. Dust with icing sugar. Makes 8 to 10 servings.

TIPS FOR CAKE BAKING

Read the recipe carefully before starting. Prepare sizes of pans called for and set aside. Remember that if the pan is too large, the cake will bake too quickly; if too small, the cake will not bake properly.

• *Do not substitute ingredients. An extra pinch of this or that will disturb a carefully balanced recipe.*

• *Ingredients should be at room temperature. Eggs separate more easily when cold, but should then be brought to room temperature before using.*

• *For maximum volume when beating egg whites, make sure the bowl and beaters have been carefully washed in warm soapy water, then rinsed and dried. Any trace of grease in the bowl or egg yolk in the whites will prevent the whites from forming stiff peaks.*

• *Measure ingredients carefully and accurately.*

• *Remember to preheat your oven before you start mixing.*

Rhubarb-and-Raspberry Platz

Platz is like coffee cake, halfway between cake and pie. It's commonly made with apples, but any combination of fruit in season can be used (berries, cherries, peaches, apricots, pears); just adjust the sugar according to the tartness of the fruit. It's wonderful served warm with whipped cream.

1-1/2 cups	all-purpose flour	375 mL
2 tsp	baking powder	10 mL
1/4 cup	granulated sugar	50 mL
1/4 cup	butter	50 mL
1	egg, beaten	1
1/2 cup	(approx) light cream	125 mL
	FILLING	
3 cups	coarsely chopped fresh rhubarb	750 mL
1 cup	fresh raspberries	250 mL
1 cup	granulated sugar	250 mL
1/4 cup	all-purpose flour	50 mL
1	egg, beaten	1
2 tbsp	butter, melted	25 mL
	TOPPING	
1 cup	all-purpose flour	250 mL
3/4 cup	granulated sugar	175 mL
1/2 tsp	baking powder	2 mL
1/4 cup	butter	50 mL
2 tbsp	light cream	25 mL

■ In bowl, mix together flour, baking powder and sugar; cut in butter finely. Combine egg and cream; stir into dry ingredients, adding a little more cream if needed, to make soft sticky dough. With floured hands, pat dough evenly into lightly greased 12- × 8-inch (3 L) or 9-inch (2.5 L) square cake pan.

■ **Filling:** In bowl, combine rhubarb, raspberries, sugar and flour. Combine egg and melted butter; gently mix into fruit mixture. Spread evenly over base in pan.

■ **Topping:** In bowl, mix together flour, sugar and baking powder; cut in butter. Stir in cream to make crumbly mixture; sprinkle over fruit.

■ Bake in 325°F (160°C) oven for 45 to 50 minutes or until golden brown. To serve, cut into large squares. Makes about 8 servings.

Black Forest Roll

Bing cherries star in this rolled version of the ever-popular party cake. It's easy to make and slices beautifully. You can make the chocolate cake and cherry syrup ahead of time and assemble the roll an hour or so before serving.

1 cup	all-purpose flour	250 mL
1/4 cup	unsweetened cocoa powder	50 mL
1 tsp	baking powder	5 mL
1/4 tsp	salt	1 mL
3	eggs	3
1 cup	granulated sugar	250 mL
3 tbsp	water	50 mL
1 tsp	vanilla	5 mL
	Icing sugar	
3 oz	semisweet chocolate, melted	90 g

CHERRY SYRUP		
4 cups	black sweet cherries	1 L
1 tbsp	water	15 mL
2 tbsp	granulated sugar	25 mL
2 tbsp	cherry liqueur or brandy (or dash almond extract)	25 mL

FILLING		
1 cup	whipping cream	250 mL
2 tbsp	icing sugar	25 mL
1/2 tsp	vanilla	2 mL

■ Stir together flour, cocoa, baking powder and salt; set aside. In mixing bowl, beat eggs until thick and lemon-colored. Gradually beat in granulated sugar. Stir in water and vanilla; gradually blend in flour mixture. Spread batter in greased and waxed paper-lined 15- × 10-inch (40 × 25 cm) jelly roll pan.

■ Bake in 375°F (190°C) oven for 10 to 12 minutes or until cake tester inserted in centre comes out clean. Invert onto tea towel dusted lightly with icing sugar; peel off paper. Starting at short end, roll up cake in towel. Let cool seam side down on rack. *(Towel-wrapped cake can be stored in large plastic bag in cool place for up to 1 day.)*

■ **Cherry Syrup:** In heavy saucepan, mash 2 cups (500 mL) of the cherries. Add water; cover and cook over very low heat for 15 to 20 minutes or until juices are released. Strain through sieve into bowl, pressing out juice. Return juice to saucepan; stir in sugar and bring to simmer. Simmer until reduced by one-third and consistency of thin syrup. Add 1 tbsp (15 mL) of the liqueur or dash of almond extract. Let cool. *(Sauce can be covered and refrigerated for up to 1 day.)*

■ Halve and pit remaining cherries; sprinkle with remaining liqueur. Stir and set aside.

■ **Filling:** Whip cream; beat in sugar and vanilla.

■ Unroll cake; brush with half of the cherry syrup. Spread with cream filling, leaving 1/2-inch (1 cm) border uncovered. Sprinkle cherries over filling. Roll up and place seam side down on serving platter. Brush with remaining syrup. Let stand for 20 minutes.

■ With spoon, drizzle chocolate over cake in crisscross pattern. Refrigerate until set or for up to 1 hour. Makes 8 servings.

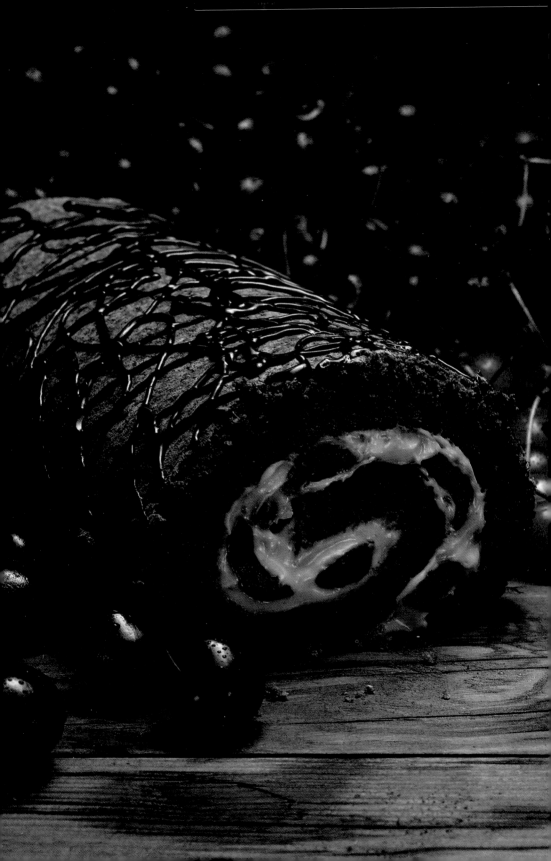

Blueberry-Lemon Picnic Cake

Take this cake along to a picnic right in the baking pan covered tightly with foil.

3/4 cup	butter	175 mL
1 cup	granulated sugar	250 mL
4	eggs	4
2 cups	all-purpose flour	500 mL
1 tbsp	baking powder	15 mL
1/2 tsp	salt	2 mL
1/4 tsp	nutmeg	1 mL
1/2 cup	milk	125 mL
2 tsp	grated lemon rind	10 mL
1 tsp	vanilla	5 mL
2 cups	blueberries	500 mL

	GLAZE	
1/2 cup	granulated sugar	125 mL
2 tbsp	lemon juice	25 mL

■ In large mixing bowl, beat butter until creamy; gradually beat in sugar, beating until consistency of thick whipped cream. Beat in eggs, one at a time, beating well after each addition.

■ Stir together flour, baking powder, salt and nutmeg; stir into creamed mixture alternately with milk. Stir in lemon rind and vanilla; fold in blueberries. Spread in greased 13- × 9-inch (3.5 L) cake pan. Bake in 350°F (180°C) oven for 40 to 45 minutes or until golden and cake tester inserted in centre comes out clean. Let stand in pan for 5 minutes.

■ **Glaze:** Meanwhile, stir together sugar and lemon juice; let stand for 20 minutes. Spoon over warm cake and spread evenly. Let cool completely in pan on rack. Makes 12 to 15 servings.

If frosting is too sweet for you, try using a lacy paper doily as a stencil and sift icing sugar on top of your cake instead. Or use your imagination and cut your own stencil . . . initials, numbers or a flower. Place the stencil on the cake; shake icing sugar through a small sieve, fairly heavily, over top. Gently remove stencil.

Chocolate Carrot Cake with Chocolate Cream Cheese Icing

To decorate this delightful cake, shape tiny carrots from marzipan and tint them with orange and green paste food colorings.

1-1/2 cups	sifted all-purpose flour	375 mL
3/4 cup	unsweetened cocoa powder	175 mL
1-1/2 tsp	baking powder	7 mL
1-1/2 tsp	cinnamon	7 mL
1 tsp	baking soda	5 mL
1/4 tsp	nutmeg	1 mL
Pinch	allspice	Pinch
1/2 cup	chopped walnuts, toasted*	125 mL
1/2 cup	raisins	125 mL
1/3 cup	sweetened flaked coconut	75 mL
3	eggs	3
3/4 cup	packed brown sugar	175 mL
3/4 cup	granulated sugar	175 mL
3/4 cup	vegetable oil	175 mL
4 oz	semisweet chocolate, melted	125 g
3 cups	grated carrots	750 mL
	ICING	
1/2 lb	cream cheese	250 g
1/4 lb	semisweet chocolate, melted	125 g
2 cups	sifted icing sugar	500 mL

■ In bowl, combine flour, cocoa, baking powder, cinnamon, baking soda, nutmeg and allspice; stir in walnuts, raisins and coconut.

■ In large bowl, beat eggs; gradually blend in brown and granulated sugars. Add oil; beat in chocolate. Stir in carrots. Add flour mixture all at once, mixing just until evenly combined.

■ Line greased 13- × 9-inch (3.5 L) cake pan with parchment paper or waxed paper. Grease paper. Pour batter into pan and bake in 325°F (160°C) oven for 35 to 40 minutes or until top springs back when lightly touched and cake begins to pull away from sides of pan. Let cool.

■ **Icing:** Meanwhile, in bowl, beat cream cheese until light; beat in chocolate. Gradually beat in sugar; cover and chill in refrigerator for 30 to 60 minutes or until spreadable. Spread over cooled cake. Makes 12 to 16 servings.
*Toast walnuts on baking sheet in 350°F (180°C) oven for about 10 minutes or until lightly browned.

Chocolate Raspberry Mousse Cake

This recipe makes double the amount of cake needed, so you'll be able to freeze the extra cake to have on hand when you want to make an encore of these fabulous flavors.

CHOCOLATE CAKE

3	eggs, separated	3
1/3 cup	granulated sugar	75 mL
1/2 cup	all-purpose flour	125 mL
2 tbsp	unsweetened cocoa powder	25 mL

RASPBERRY SYRUP

1/4 cup	granulated sugar	50 mL
1/4 cup	water	50 mL
2 tbsp	raspberry liqueur	25 mL

RASPBERRY MOUSSE

1-1/2	pkg unflavored gelatin	1-1/2
1/4 cup	water	50 mL
2	pkg (each 300 g) frozen raspberries, thawed	2
3/4 cup	granulated sugar	175 mL
2 tbsp	lemon juice	25 mL
2 tbsp	raspberry liqueur	25 mL
2 cups	whipping cream	500 mL

CHOCOLATE GLAZE

4 oz	semisweet chocolate	125 g
1/4 cup	whipping cream	50 mL

■ **Chocolate Cake:** In large bowl, beat egg yolks with 1/4 cup (50 mL) of the sugar until very pale. In separate bowl, beat egg whites until soft peaks form; gradually beat in remaining sugar until stiff peaks form. Fold egg white mixture into egg yolk mixture.

■ Sift flour and cocoa over egg mixture; gently fold in. Pour into buttered 8-inch (2 L) springform pan; bake in 350°F (180°C) oven for 30 to 35 minutes or until top springs back when lightly touched. Run knife around edge of cake to loosen. Let cool on wire rack.

■ **Raspberry Syrup:** In small saucepan, combine sugar and water; cook over medium heat until sugar has dissolved, about 1 minute. Stir in liqueur. Let cool.

■ **Raspberry Mousse:** In small saucepan, sprinkle gelatin over water; let stand for 5 minutes to soften. Pass berries through food mill to purée and remove seeds to make about 2 cups (500 mL). (Alternatively, in blender or food processor, purée berries, then press through sieve.)

■ Transfer purée to separate saucepan. Add sugar and lemon juice; cook over medium heat, stirring occasionally, until sugar has dissolved, about 5 minutes. Stir in liqueur; transfer to large bowl.

■ Over low heat, heat gelatin until dissolved; stir into raspberry mixture. Chill, stirring occasionally, over larger bowl of ice and water for about 20 minutes or until consistency of raw egg whites. Whip cream; fold into cooled raspberry mixture. Reserve 1/2 cup (125 mL) for garnish.

■ To assemble, cut cake into 3 or 4 thin layers; reserve 2 layers and freeze remaining layers for another use. Sprinkle 1 cut side of each of the 2 layers with raspberry syrup. Place 1 layer, syrup side up, in 9-inch (2.5 L) springform pan; pour in half of the raspberry mousse. Top with second cake layer; pour in enough of the remaining mousse to come almost to top of pan. Smooth surface. Refrigerate until firm, 1 to 2 hours.

■ **Chocolate Glaze:** In top of double boiler over hot, not boiling, water, melt chocolate with cream, stirring until smooth. Let cool to room temperature yet still spreadable; pour over mousse and spread evenly. Spoon remaining mousse into pastry bag fitted with small plain tip; pipe three concentric circles over top of cake. Pull toothpick through circles to form spiderweb design. Refrigerate until chilled.

Chocolate Raspberry Mousse Cake;
Dark Chocolate Soufflé Cake with
White Chocolate Fluff (p. 46) ▲

Dark Chocolate Soufflé Cake with White Chocolate Fluff

A cooled soufflé deflates into a wonderful cake. Here, white chocolate mousse is mounded on top, then decorated with two-color curls.

SOUFFLÉ CAKE		
6 oz	semisweet chocolate, chopped	175 g
1/3 cup	unsalted butter	75 mL
6	eggs, separated	6
2 tbsp	granulated sugar	25 mL

WHITE CHOCOLATE FLUFF		
8 oz	white chocolate, chopped	250 g
2 cups	whipping cream	500 mL

GARNISH		
2 oz	each semisweet chocolate and white chocolate (at room temperature)	60 g

■ **Soufflé Cake:** Line well-buttered 9-inch (2.5 L) springform pan with circle of waxed paper; butter again and set aside.

■ In top of double boiler over hot, not boiling, water, melt chocolate with butter, stirring until smooth. Beat in egg yolks. In bowl, beat egg whites until soft peaks form; beat in sugar until stiff peaks form. Fold into chocolate mixture. Spoon gently into prepared pan.

■ Bake in 400°F (200°C) oven for 10 minutes. Reduce heat to 350°F (180°C) and bake for 20 minutes longer or until puffed. Let cool. Run knife around edge of cooled cake; remove ring. Invert onto serving platter; carefully remove paper.

■ **White Chocolate Fluff:** Meanwhile, place white chocolate in bowl. In small saucepan over medium heat, scald 1/2 cup (125 mL) of the cream until tiny bubbles form around edge of pan; pour over chocolate and stir until melted. Stir in remaining cream. Chill. Beat until fluffy and soft peaks form. Spoon or pipe over cake.

■ **Garnish:** Dip swivel vegetable peeler into boiling water and dry; peel off dark and white chocolate curls onto waxed paper. Scatter over top of cake. Refrigerate for 2 hours before serving.

Strawberries-and-Cream Cake

This new version of an old classic is based on a génoise (a buttery sponge cake) rather than a shortcake.

6	eggs (at room temperature)	6
1 cup	granulated sugar	250 mL
1 tsp	vanilla	5 mL
1 cup	cake-and-pastry flour	250 mL
1/2 tsp	baking powder	2 mL
1/3 cup	butter, melted and cooled until lukewarm	75 mL
	FILLING	
2 cups	whipping cream	500 mL
2 tbsp	granulated sugar	25 mL
1/2 tsp	vanilla	2 mL
2 cups	strawberries, sliced	500 mL
	GARNISH	
	Whole strawberries	
	Chocolate-dipped strawberries (optional)	
1 oz	semisweet chocolate, melted	30 g

■ Grease 13- × 9-inch (3.5 L) cake pan. Line with waxed paper and grease again.

■ Rinse mixing bowl in hot water and wipe dry. Add eggs and beat until foamy; gradually beat in sugar. Beat at high speed for 8 to 10 minutes or until thick, pale yellow and tripled in volume. Beat in vanilla.

■ Sift together flour and baking powder; lightly fold into batter. Fold in butter. Pour into prepared pan. Bake in 325°F (160°C) oven for 25 to 30 minutes or until cake springs bake when lightly touched in centre. Turn cake out onto rack; remove paper and let cool. Cut cake in half lengthwise; cut halves horizontally to make total of 4 layers.

■ **Filling:** Whip cream; beat in sugar and vanilla. Set 1 cup (250 mL) aside. Fold strawberries into remaining cream. Assemble cake, spreading one-third of the filling over each layer.

■ **Garnish:** Top cake with reserved whipped cream. Decorate with whole berries, and chocolate-coated berries (if using). Drizzle with melted chocolate. Makes about 8 servings.

Chocolate Bread Pudding with Grand Marnier Custard Sauce

If you enjoy old-fashioned bread pudding, try this creamy chocolate version. It's baked covered to prevent the chocolate from burning.

8	slices egg bread, crusts removed	8
1/3 cup	unsalted butter, melted	75 mL
1-1/2 cups	light cream or milk	375 mL
1 cup	milk	250 mL
6 oz	semisweet chocolate, chopped	175 g
3	eggs	3
3	egg yolks	3
1/2 cup	granulated sugar	125 mL
1 tsp	vanilla	5 mL
	Grand Marnier Custard Sauce (recipe follows)	

■ Brush both sides of bread slices with butter; place on baking sheet. Bake in 400°F (200°C) oven until golden brown, 3 to 5 minutes per side.

■ In heavy saucepan, heat cream and milk over medium-high heat until bubbles form at edge. Remove from heat; stir in chocolate until smooth.

■ In bowl, whisk together eggs, yolks and sugar; stir in chocolate mixture and vanilla.

■ Arrange bread in 9-inch (2.5 L) square baking dish; pour custard over. Cover surface of pudding with plastic wrap. Place slightly smaller dish on top and weigh down with heavy cans. Let pudding stand for 30 minutes.

■ Remove weights and plastic wrap. Cover dish with foil and puncture with fork for steam vents.

■ Place dish in larger shallow baking dish. Pour in enough boiling water to reach halfway up sides of dish. Bake in 325°F (160°C) oven until firm, about 1 hour and 15 minutes. Let cool for at least 30 minutes before serving. *(Pudding can be covered and refrigerated overnight. Reheat gently or serve cold.)*

■ To serve, cut pudding into squares. Spoon a little Grand Marnier Custard Sauce on each plate; top with square. Pour more sauce over if desired. Makes 8 servings.

GRAND MARNIER CUSTARD SAUCE

2	egg yolks	2
1/3 cup	granulated sugar	75 mL
2 tsp	all-purpose flour	10 mL
1 cup	milk	250 mL
1/2 cup	light cream	125 mL
2 tbsp	Grand Marnier or other orange liqueur	25 mL

■ In mixing bowl, beat together egg yolks, sugar and flour until light and lemon colored. In saucepan, heat milk with cream until bubbles form around edge of pan; beat into yolk mixture. Transfer to saucepan; cook gently over low heat, stirring constantly, until custard has thickened. Stir in liqueur. Serve warm or cold. Makes about 1-1/2 cups (375 mL).

Plum Cobbler

Good old-fashioned desserts like this one bring back thoughts of family and friends gathered at the table. It's delicious served on its own or with cream.

4 cups	quartered prune plums	1 L
3/4 cup	granulated sugar	175 mL
1/3 cup	orange juice	75 mL
2 tbsp	quick-cooking tapioca	25 mL
1-1/2 cups	all-purpose flour	375 mL
2 tbsp	(approx) granulated sugar	25 mL
1 tbsp	baking powder	15 mL
1/2 tsp	salt	2 mL
3 tbsp	butter or shortening	50 mL
2 tbsp	flaked coconut	25 mL
2 tsp	grated orange rind	10 mL
2/3 cup	milk	150 mL

■ Place plums in well-buttered 11- × 7-inch (2 L) baking dish. Mix together 3/4 cup (175 mL) sugar, orange juice and tapioca; drizzle over fruit and set aside.

■ In bowl, stir together flour, 2 tbsp (25 mL) sugar, baking powder and salt; cut in butter until mixture resembles fine crumbs. Stir in coconut and orange rind. With fork, lightly mix in milk to make soft dough.

■ Turn out onto floured board; gently knead 12 times. Roll or pat into rectangle slightly smaller than dish; cut into 6 or 8 squares or rounds. Cut small cross in centre of each square; arrange over fruit. Sprinkle with sugar.

■ Bake in 400°F (200°C) oven for about 25 minutes or until topping is browned and fruit is bubbling. Makes 6 to 8 servings.

Strawberries au Gratin

This rich sabayon is spooned over fresh strawberries, then broiled until lightly browned — classic simplicity at its best.

2 cups	strawberries	500 mL
	Pepper	
4	egg yolks	4
1/2 cup	instant dissolving (fruit/berry) sugar	125 mL
1/2 cup	dry white wine	125 mL

■ Halve strawberries lengthwise; arrange in single layer in ovenproof au gratin dish. Sprinkle with pepper to taste; set aside.

■ In heavy saucepan or top of double boiler, combine egg yolks, sugar and wine; cook over medium heat, whisking constantly, for 6 to 8 minutes or until sauce coats back of spoon.

■ Spoon sauce over strawberries; broil for 1 to 2 minutes or until golden brown. Makes 4 servings.

Plum Cobbler ▶

Buttered Rum Fondue

Serve this fabulous fondue with peach and pear wedges, grapes, apple chunks, pineapple spears and bite-size pieces of pound cake or ladyfingers.

1/4 cup	butter	50 mL	
3/4 cup	lightly packed brown sugar	175 mL	
2 tbsp	corn syrup	25 mL	
1/4 cup	whipping cream	50 mL	
2 tbsp	rum (or 1/2 tsp/2 mL rum extract)	25 mL	
	Fresh fruit chunks (at room temperature)		

■ In saucepan, melt butter over medium heat; stir in sugar and corn syrup until sugar is dissolved. Add cream and bring to simmer, stirring; remove from heat. Add rum; let cool to dipping consistency. Transfer to fondue pot and set over warmer. Skewer fruit and dip into sauce. Makes about 1 cup (250 mL) sauce.

Fast Chocolate Fondue

This takes less than 10 minutes to make. Be careful and stir it often because chocolate burns easily.

1/2 lb	milk chocolate	250 g
1 oz	unsweetened chocolate	30 g
1/2 cup	light cream	125 mL
1/4 cup	coffee liqueur	50 mL
	Fresh fruit chunks	

■ In fondue pot over low heat, melt together milk chocolate and unsweetened chocolate. Gradually stir in cream, then liqueur until smooth. Skewer fruit and dip into sauce. Makes about 1 cup (250 mL) sauce.

> FONDUE DIPPERS
>
> *A fondue is an informal and fun way to serve dessert. Be sure to provide a variety of fondue dippers for your guests. Choose from strawberries, peach or pear wedges, seedless grapes, apple or pineapple chunks, bananas, orange sections, kiwi slices, maraschino cherries, angel cake cubes, pound cake cubes, lady fingers or marshmallows.*

Quick Dessert Crêpes

Make the batter in minutes, cook the crêpes and serve immediately. Or freeze a batch of crêpes between layers of waxed paper; thaw and heat to serve with suggested sauces or your favorite topping. Honey, fruit preserves, chocolate sauce and apple butter are delicious choices.

1 cup	all-purpose flour	250 mL
1 tbsp	granulated sugar	15 mL
1/4 tsp	salt	1 mL
1-1/2 cups	milk	375 mL
2	eggs	2
1/3 cup	butter, melted	75 mL
	Berry Raspberry Sauce or Blueberry Lemon Sauce (recipes follow)	

■ In bowl, stir together flour, sugar and salt. Blend together milk, eggs and 1/4 cup (50 mL) of the butter; whisk into dry ingredients, blending well.

■ In 8-inch (20 cm) crêpe pan, heat a little of the remaining butter over medium heat; do not allow to burn. Pour 2 tbsp (25 mL) batter into pan and swirl quickly to coat bottom. Cook for 30 to 50 seconds or until bottom is lightly browned.

■ Flip crêpe or turn gently with spatula; cook for 25 seconds longer. Transfer to heated plate. Repeat with remaining batter, brushing pan with a little of the melted butter before cooking each crêpe. To serve, fold crêpes into thirds, browned side out; drizzle with sauce. Makes 12 crêpes.

BERRY RASPBERRY SAUCE

1	pkg (300 g) frozen unsweetened raspberries, thawed	1
3 tbsp	strawberry jam	50 mL
2 tbsp	granulated sugar	25 mL

■ In food processor or blender, purée raspberries. Over saucepan, press purée through sieve to remove seeds. Add jam and sugar; heat until bubbly, about 5 minutes. Serve warm, at room temperature or cold. Makes 1 cup (250 mL).

BLUEBERRY LEMON SAUCE

1/2 cup	cold water	125 mL
1/3 cup	granulated sugar	75 mL
1 tbsp	cornstarch	15 mL
1 cup	frozen unsweetened blueberries	250 mL
1/2 tsp	grated lemon rind	2 mL
1 tbsp	lemon juice	15 mL

■ In small saucepan, mix water, sugar and cornstarch until smooth. Add blueberries, lemon rind and lemon juice; cook over medium heat until bubbly and thickened, about 10 minutes. Makes about 1 cup (250 mL).

Hot Chocolate Soufflé with Coffee Sauce

Here's a chocolate lover's dream come true. Use a good-quality coffee ice cream for the sauce.

6 oz	semisweet chocolate, chopped	175 g
1/3 cup	unsalted butter	75 mL
6	eggs, separated	6
1/4 tsp	cream of tartar	1 mL
3 tbsp	granulated sugar	50 mL
	SAUCE	
2 cups	coffee ice cream	500 mL
2 tbsp	dark rum or coffee liqueur (optional)	25 mL
	GARNISH	
	Strawberries (optional)	
	Sifted icing sugar	

■ In double boiler over hot, not boiling, water, melt chocolate with butter. Remove from heat and beat in egg yolks. Transfer to large bowl; whisk until slightly cooled.

■ In separate bowl, beat egg whites with cream of tartar until soft peaks form. Beat in sugar, 1 tbsp (15 mL) at a time, until stiff peaks form; stir one-quarter into chocolate mixture. Gently fold in remaining egg white mixture.

■ Dust well-buttered 8-cup (2 L) soufflé dish with granulated sugar; spoon in chocolate mixture. *(Soufflé can be prepared to this point and kept at room temperature for up to 1 hour.)* Bake in 425°F (220°C) oven for 5 minutes. Reduce heat to 400°F (200°C) and bake for 15 to 20 minutes longer or until puffy and almost firm to the touch.

■ **Sauce:** Meanwhile, melt ice cream completely; stir in rum (if using). Garnish with strawberries (if using). Sprinkle soufflé with icing sugar and serve immediately. Spoon sauce over. Makes 8 to 10 servings.

Snow Pudding with Tropical Fruit Sauce

This baked pudding has the light texture of a sponge cake. It's best served warm rather than hot.

1-1/4 cups	sifted cake-and-pastry flour	300 mL
2 tsp	baking powder	10 mL
1/4 tsp	salt	1 mL
Pinch	mace	Pinch
1/2 cup	granulated sugar	125 mL
3 tbsp	vegetable oil	50 mL
2	egg yolks	2
2 tbsp	water	25 mL
	Grated rind and juice of 1 lime	
3	egg whites	3
	SAUCE	
1	can (14 oz/398 mL) pineapple chunks	1
1 tsp	cornstarch	5 mL
2	tangerines	2
1	mango, peeled and cut in chunks	1

■ Stir together flour, baking powder, salt and mace; set aside. In large bowl, blend together sugar, oil, egg yolks, water, lime rind and juice; stir in flour mixture, blending well.

■ In bowl, beat egg whites until stiff peaks form; stir about 1 cup (250 mL) into batter. Fold in remaining egg whites. Pour into ungreased 6-cup (1.5 L) tube pan. Bake in 350°F (180°C) oven for 30 to 35 minutes or until top is golden and springs back when touched. Invert pan and let hang for 5 minutes so that cake doesn't touch anything.

■ **Sauce:** Drain juice from pineapple into small saucepan; set fruit aside. Stir in cornstarch. Squeeze juice from 1 of the tangerines and add to pan. Finely chop 1 tsp (5 mL) tangerine rind and stir into pan. Peel, section and remove membrane from remaining tangerine, adding any juices to pan; reserve a few sections for garnish.

■ Bring juice mixture to simmer; cook, stirring, until thickened and clear. Reduce heat to medium-low and cook for 3 minutes longer. Gently stir in pineapple, tangerine sections and mango; heat, stirring, just until warm.

■ Spoon about 2 tbsp (25 mL) sauce around edge of pudding; run knife around edge and turn out onto deep-rimmed plate. Spoon remaining sauce in centre and over top. Garnish with reserved tangerine sections. Makes about 8 servings.

Cherry Crumble

Chopped pecans add a delicious crunch to this easy-to-make old-fashioned fruit crumble. Serve warm with cream or ice cream.

3 cups	pitted sour cherries	750 mL
1/2 cup	granulated sugar	125 mL
1 tbsp	quick-cooking tapioca	15 mL
1 cup	rolled oats (not instant)	250 mL
1/2 cup	packed brown sugar	125 mL
1/4 cup	all-purpose flour	50 mL
1/4 cup	chopped pecans	50 mL
1/4 tsp	salt	1 mL
Pinch	each cloves and nutmeg	Pinch
1/2 cup	butter	125 mL

■ In 8-inch (2 L) square cake pan, mix together cherries, granulated sugar and tapioca; set aside.

■ In bowl, stir together rolled oats, brown sugar, flour, pecans, salt, cloves and nutmeg. With pastry blender or two knives, cut in butter until mixture is crumbly; sprinkle over cherries. Bake in 375°F (190°C) oven for 35 to 40 minutes or until top is golden and cherries are bubbling. Serve warm. Makes about 8 servings.

Warm Plum Compote

Large purple plums are wonderful in compotes. You can also make delectable variations by combining plums, apples and pears.

3 cups	unsweetened apple juice	750 mL
1	stick (2 inches/5 cm) cinnamon (or 1/2 tsp/2 mL ground)	1
3	whole cloves	3
1 tsp	grated lemon rind	5 mL
6	plums, halved and pitted (1 lb/500 g)	6

■ In saucepan, bring apple juice, cinnamon, cloves and lemon rind to boil. Reduce heat to medium and add plums; poach gently, spooning liquid over and turning plums once, for 5 to 8 minutes or until tender.

■ With slotted spoon, remove plums and keep warm. Increase heat to high; boil liquid for 10 minutes or until syrupy. Strain and spoon over plums. Makes 4 servings.

Sherried Pears Jubilee

Serve this deliciously rich concoction in pretty glasses and garnish with candied violets, or spoon it over cold, creamy vanilla ice cream.

3 cups	water	750 mL
1 cup	granulated sugar	250 mL
	Rind of 1 lemon (yellow part only)	
5	pears	5
1/2 cup	butter	125 mL
2/3 cup	dry sherry	150 mL
1/2 cup	packed light brown sugar	125 mL
2 tbsp	lemon juice	25 mL
1 tbsp	cornstarch	15 mL
1/4 cup	golden raisins	50 mL
1/4 cup	brandy (optional)	50 mL

■ In large saucepan, combine water and granulated sugar; cook over high heat, stirring, until sugar has dissolved. Add lemon rind; reduce heat to simmer.

■ Peel, core and cut pears into quarters. Add to pan and cook over low heat just until tender, 5 to 7 minutes. Drain and set pears aside; discard lemon rind.

■ In saucepan, melt butter over low heat; stir in sherry, brown sugar, lemon juice and cornstarch. Bring to simmer over medium-high heat. Reduce heat to medium; add raisins and simmer gently for 5 minutes. Add pears, stirring gently to coat. Transfer to serving bowl. Warm brandy (if using) in small saucepan over low heat; carefully ignite and pour over pears. Makes about 6 servings.

Rhubarb Crisp

Granola and chopped pecans make this all-time favorite dessert extra crisp. It's delicious served warm with cream or ice cream.

4 cups	coarsely chopped rhubarb	1 L
1-1/4 cups	all-purpose flour	300 mL
1/4 cup	granulated sugar	50 mL
1/2 cup	strawberry jam	125 mL
1-1/2 cups	granola	375 mL
1/2 tsp	cinnamon	2 mL
1/2 tsp	ginger	2 mL
1/2 cup	packed brown sugar	125 mL
1/2 cup	chopped pecans	125 mL
1/2 cup	butter, softened	125 mL

■ In bowl, combine rhubarb, 1/4 cup (50 mL) of the flour and granulated sugar. Stir in jam; set aside.

■ In separate bowl, combine remaining flour, granola, cinnamon and ginger. Stir in brown sugar and pecans; blend in butter until crumbly.

■ Press 2 cups (500 mL) of the granola mixture into bottom of 8-inch (2 L) square baking dish. Spoon rhubarb mixture over top; cover evenly with remaining granola mixture. Bake in 375°F (190°C) oven for 40 to 50 minutes or until deep golden brown and filling is tender. Makes about 8 servings.

Hot Buttered Pineapple

Here's a dessert to bake along with supper. Served topped with ice cream, it's an upside-down pineapple sundae! And so convenient — it bakes while you're eating dinner.

1	small pineapple	1
1/4 cup	maple syrup	50 mL
2 tbsp	rum (optional)	25 mL
2 tbsp	butter	25 mL
	Whipped cream or ice cream (optional)	

■ Cut top from pineapple; peel, core and cut into chunks. Place in 8-cup (2 L) baking dish. Drizzle with maple syrup, and rum (if using); dot with butter.

■ Cover tightly and bake in 375°F (190°C) oven for 20 to 30 minutes or until hot and bubbling. Serve topped with whipped cream (if using). Makes 4 to 6 servings.

Broiled Orange Halves

Enjoy sweet and succulent winter oranges with a scoop of ice cream on the side if you like.

2	large seedless oranges	2
2 tsp	packed brown sugar	10 mL
2 tsp	butter, melted	10 mL
1/4 tsp	vanilla or rum extract	1 mL

■ Cut oranges in half crosswise. Using serrated knife, cut around pulp to separate from membranes and peel, leaving pulp in peel. Place, cut sides up, in shallow baking dish. Combine sugar, butter and vanilla; spread over oranges. Broil for 2 to 4 minutes or until hot and bubbling. Makes 4 servings.

Butterscotch Sauce

A great sauce for vanilla ice cream.

1 cup	packed brown sugar	250 mL
1/2 cup	corn syrup	125 mL
1/4 cup	butter	50 mL
2 tbsp	water	25 mL
1 tbsp	vanilla	15 mL
1/2 cup	whipping cream	125 mL

■ In heavy saucepan, bring sugar, corn syrup, butter and water to boil over medium-high heat, stirring constantly; boil for 1 minute. Reduce heat to medium and cook for 5 minutes. Remove from heat and stir in vanilla. Let cool slightly. Stir in cream. (Sauce thickens as it cools.) Makes 1-1/2 cups (375 mL).

Super Chocolate Sauce

This is great on almost any ice cream.

3 oz	semisweet chocolate	90 g
1/4 cup	unsalted butter	50 mL
1 tbsp	dark rum (optional)	15 mL
1 tbsp	strong coffee	15 mL
1 cup	icing sugar	250 mL
3/4 cup	evaporated milk	175 mL
1 tsp	vanilla	5 mL

■ In heavy saucepan over medium heat, combine chocolate, butter, rum (if using) and coffee; heat just until chocolate has melted. Remove from heat; whisk in sugar and milk.

■ Return to heat and slowly bring to boil; cook, stirring constantly, for about 5 minutes or until thick and creamy. Remove from heat; stir in vanilla. (Sauce thickens as it cools.) Makes 1 cup (250 mL).

Apricot Pecan Sauce

For a fabulous fast dessert, spoon this spirited sauce over vanilla or butter-pecan ice cream, or pound or sponge cake.

1/2 cup	apricot jam or preserve	125 mL
1/2 cup	whipping cream	125 mL
1/2 cup	chopped pecans, toasted*	125 mL
2 tbsp	butter	25 mL
2 tbsp	rum	25 mL
1/2 tsp	vanilla	2 mL

■ In saucepan, combine apricot jam and cream; bring to boil. Reduce heat and cook gently, stirring, for 2 to 3 minutes or until blended. Stir in nuts, butter, rum and vanilla. Serve warm or at room temperature. Makes about 1 cup (250 mL).

*Bake pecans on baking sheet in 350°F (180°C) oven for 10 minutes or until lightly toasted.

Super Chocolate Sauce ▶

Credits

Recipes in THE CANADIAN LIVING COOKING COLLECTION have been created by the *Canadian Living* Test Kitchen and by the following food writers from across Canada: **Elizabeth Baird, Karen Brown, Joanna Burkhard, James Chatto, Diane Clement, David Cohlmeyer, Pam Collacott, Bonnie Baker Cowan, Pierre Dubrulle, Eileen Dwillies, Nancy Enright, Carol Ferguson, Margaret Fraser, Susan Furlan, Anita Goldberg, Barb Holland, Patricia Jamieson, Arlene Lappin, Anne Lindsay, Lispeth Lodge, Mary McGrath, Susan Mendelson, Bernard Meyer, Beth Moffatt, Rose Murray, Iris Raven, Gerry Shikatani, Jill Snider, Kay Spicer, Linda Stephen, Bonnie Stern, Lucy Waverman, Carol White, Ted Whittaker** and **Cynny Willet.**

The full-color photographs throughout are by Canada's leading food photographers, including **Fred Bird, Doug Bradshaw, Christopher Campbell, Nino D'Angelo, Frank Grant, Michael Kohn, Suzanne McCormick, Claude Noel, John Stephens** and **Mike Visser.**

Editorial and Production Staff: Hugh Brewster, Susan Barrable, Catherine Fraccaro, Wanda Nowakowska, Sandra L. Hall, Beverley Renahan and Bernice Eisenstein.

Index

LOOK FOR THESE BESTSELLING COOKBOOKS FROM *CANADIAN LIVING*

The most trusted name in Canadian cooking

New this Fall!
CANADIAN LIVING'S COUNTRY COOKING
Rediscover the familiar tastes of country cooking at its comforting best in the pages of this beautiful full-color cookbook. Each of the more than 200 dishes featured here is brimming over with flavor and honest, great taste....*$27.00 hardcover*

THE CANADIAN LIVING COOKBOOK
Beautiful yet practical, this Canadian classic features over 525 recipes by Canada's finest food writers and a host of cooking hints, charts and ideas....*$35.00 hardcover*

THE CANADIAN LIVING LIGHT & HEALTHY COOKBOOK
Over 150 nutritious *and* delicious recipes make it easy to prepare healthy, balanced meals for the whole family. Includes handy nutrition charts for each recipe plus health and food facts....*$20.00 softcover*

THE CANADIAN LIVING MICROWAVE COOKBOOK
Over 175 delicious recipes — plus microwaving basics, charts and tips — make this an invaluable book no microwave owner should be without....*$27.00 hardcover*

THE CANADIAN LIVING RUSH-HOUR COOKBOOK
This easy-to-use cookbook features over 200 recipes and 100 menus for fast and tasty everyday meals that can be prepared in under 60 minutes. A must for today's busy cooks....*$27.00 hardcover*

THE CANADIAN LIVING BARBECUE COOKBOOK
Over 175 tested recipes for easy and delicious summer cooking plus the latest information on barbecue equipment and techniques....*$19.95 softcover*

THE CANADIAN LIVING ENTERTAINING COOKBOOK
A gorgeous gift book featuring over 350 easy-to-prepare recipes for every entertaining occasion. It includes inventive menus plus the latest ideas for setting the table — and the mood!...*$34.95 hardcover*

Also from Canadian Living
GLORIOUS CHRISTMAS CRAFTS
Over 135 imaginative ways to make Christmas extra special....*$24.95 hardcover*

All of these full-color *Canadian Living* books are available from Random House Canada in bookstores and major department stores. To order directly from *Canadian Living*, please send a cheque or money order (payable to *Canadian Living*) for the cover price (above), plus $3 shipping and handling and 7% GST on the total amount, to: *Canadian Living*, Box 220, Oakville, Ontario L6J 5A2.